World in Focus
Japan

CELIA TIDMARSH

WAYLAND

First published in 2006 by Wayland,
an imprint of Hachette Children's Books

© Wayland 2006

Commissioning editor: Victoria Brooker
Editor: Patience Coster
Inside design: Chris Halls, www.mindseyedesign.co.uk
Cover design: Wayland

Series concept and project management by EASI-Educational Resourcing
(info@easi-er.co.uk)
Statistical research: Anna Bowden
Maps and graphs: Martin Darlison, Encompass Graphics

British Library Cataloguing in Publication Data
Tidmarsh, Celia
   Japan. - (World in focus)
   1.Japan - Juvenile literature
   I. Title
   952'.05

ISBN-10: 075024688X
ISBN-13: 9780750246880

Printed and bound in China

Wayland
A division of Hachette Children's Books
338 Euston Road, London NW1 3BH

Cover top: Mount Fuji, a symbol of Japan and one of its most popular attractions.
Cover bottom: Kabuki theatre actors create and apply their own make-up according to traditional methods.
Title page: The Meiji shrine in Tokyo, built in memory of Emperor Meiji and Empress Shoken and completed in 1920.

Picture acknowledgements. The author and publisher would like to thank the following for allowing their pictures to be
reproduced in this publication:
Corbis 4 and *cover top* (Jose Fuste Raga), 6 (Robert Essel NYC), 9 (Asian Art & Archaeology Inc.), 12 (Eriko
Sugita/Reuters), 13 (Bettmann), 14 (Michael S. Yamashita), 15 (Wolfgang Kaehler), 16 (Michael S. Yamashita), 17 (Issei
Kato/Reuters), 23 (Issei Kato/Reuters), 28 (Michael S. Yamashita), 32 (Steve Raymer), 33 (Kimimasa Mayama/Reuters), 37
(Stephane Reix/Photo & Co.), 44 (Richard T. Nowitz), 45 (Tom Wagner), 52 (Roger Ressmeyer), 54 (Michael S. Yamashita),
57 (Joel W. Rogers), 58 (Photowood Inc.); EASI-Images/Rob Bowden 5, 8, 10 and *title page*, 11, 18, 19, 20, 21, 22, 24, 25, 26,
27, 29, 30, 31, 34, 35, 36, 38, 39, 40, 41, 42, 43, 46, 47, 48, 49 and *cover bottom*, 50, 51, 53, 55, 56, 59.

The website addresses (URLs) included in this book were valid at the time of going to press. However, because of the
nature of the Internet, it is possible that some addresses may have changed, or sites may have changed or closed down
since publication. While the author and Publishers regret any inconvenience this may cause the readers, no responsibility
for any such changes can be accepted by either the author or the Publisher.

The directional arrow portrayed on the map on page 7 provides only an approximation of north.

The data used to produce the graphics and data panels in this title were the latest available at the time of production.

CONTENTS

CHAPTER 1

Japan – An Overview

The country of Japan lies off the eastern coast of the Asian landmass. It is an archipelago of more than 6,800 islands, with the four islands of Hokkaido, Honshu, Shikoku and Kyushu making up 98 per cent of the total land area. The land surface area is 374,744 sq km (144,689 sq miles), slightly smaller than the state of California in the USA. Japan is called Nippon (or Nihon) in Japanese, meaning 'the source of the sun'.

Japan is a rugged country. Over 75 per cent of the land area is mountainous or hilly terrain. In the past, the diversity of climatic types and habitats supported a rich variety of wildlife, but many species have been lost because of urbanization, deforestation and overfishing.

Japan lies in one of world's most seismically active regions and is prone to earthquakes. There are 77 active and many dormant volcanoes, including Mount Fuji which, at 3,776 m (12,388 ft), is the highest mountain in Japan.

PEOPLE AND HISTORY

Less than 2 per cent of Japan's population is from ethnic groups other than Japanese. Human settlement is concentrated in the flatter coastal plains, and these regions have one of the highest population densities in the world.

▼ Mount Fuji is a perfect conical volcano. It has become a symbol of Japan and is one of its most popular attractions.

The majority of the population lives in huge urban areas. There are twelve cities with more than one million inhabitants, which together make up 21 per cent of Japan's population. Tokyo is the largest city, with more than 8 million people in its central districts and more than 35 million in the wider Tokyo urban area.

Historically, Japan has experienced periods of contact with the outside world and periods of isolation from it. The influence of China dates from the fourth century and includes language, religion and architectural styles. Contact with the West dates from the 1500s, when trade links were developed, particularly with Portugal, the Netherlands and Britain. However, in 1639 isolation was imposed by Tokugawa Iemitsu (shogun at the time) and maintained for more than two hundred years. In the mid-1800s renewed contact led to the adoption of many Western institutions in the fields of law, government and the military, which helped transform the Empire of Japan into a world power. There followed several decades of Japanese expansionism into neighbouring Asia (China and Korea especially) that led to military conflicts with China and Russia between 1894 and 1905. In the twentieth century, it also led to Japan's involvement in two world wars.

ECONOMIC SUCCESS

Between the 1960s and 1980s, Japan experienced remarkable economic growth in spite of a lack of raw materials and a legacy of industrial destruction from the Second World War. Japan's factories had been targeted for bombing by the Allied forces during the war; but a hard-working and highly skilled workforce had helped bring about an extraordinary economic recovery. Despite a decade of recession during the 1990s, Japan is still the second largest economy in the world and home to many of its most successful companies, including Sony, Mitsubishi, Toyota and Canon. Such companies have produced a range of high-tech goods that have shaped the lifestyles of people in many countries. These goods include personal computers, mobile phones, game consoles and music players.

Did you know?

Tokyo is often cited as the largest city in the world, with a population of over 35 million, but this figure actually refers to Tokyo's metropolitan area, which includes the adjoining prefectures (political districts) of Chiba, Saitama and Kanagawa.

▼ The Shinjuku district of Tokyo is a prime example of Japan's economic success. Its busy neon-lit centre comes alive in the evening, as people shop and dine on their way home.

◀ Beyond Japan's cities there is evidence of a lifestyle that has changed relatively little in hundreds of years. Farming is still important and rice is a major crop. Here it is being dried near Wakayama on Honshu.

ENVIRONMENTAL CHALLENGES

The rapid pace of industrialization and population pressures have created many environmental challenges, including overcrowding and pollution. The Japanese have developed a range of strategies to cope with the increasing spread of urban and industrial areas. These strategies include the reclamation of land from the sea. Extensive pollution has caused considerable damage to human health and to the environment. Pollution problems are being tackled, with a degree of success, but some, such as the disposal of nuclear waste and dioxins, continue to cause concern.

CULTURE AND POLITICS

Japan is a modern and economically developed society, but it also maintains many cultural traditions, including the celebration of long established festivals such as *O-bon* in August. Contemporary cultural interests include reading *manga* (comic strips) and watching *animes* (animated feature films and TV shows), both of which are produced in Japan.

As a member of the G8 (a group of the eight leading industrialized nations in the world), Japan occupies a powerful position in global politics. Also, its relations with countries such as China, South Korea and North Korea are vital to the stability of South-east Asia.

Physical geography

- Land area: 374,744 sq km/144,689 sq miles
- Water area: 3,091 sq km/1,193 sq miles
- Total area: 377,835 sq km/145,882 sq miles
- World rank (by area): 61
- Land boundaries: 0 km/0 miles
- Border countries: None
- Coastline: 29,751 km/18,475 miles
- Highest point: Mount Fuji (3,776 m/ 12,388 ft)
- Lowest point: Hachiro-Gata (-4 m/-13 ft)

Source: CIA World Factbook

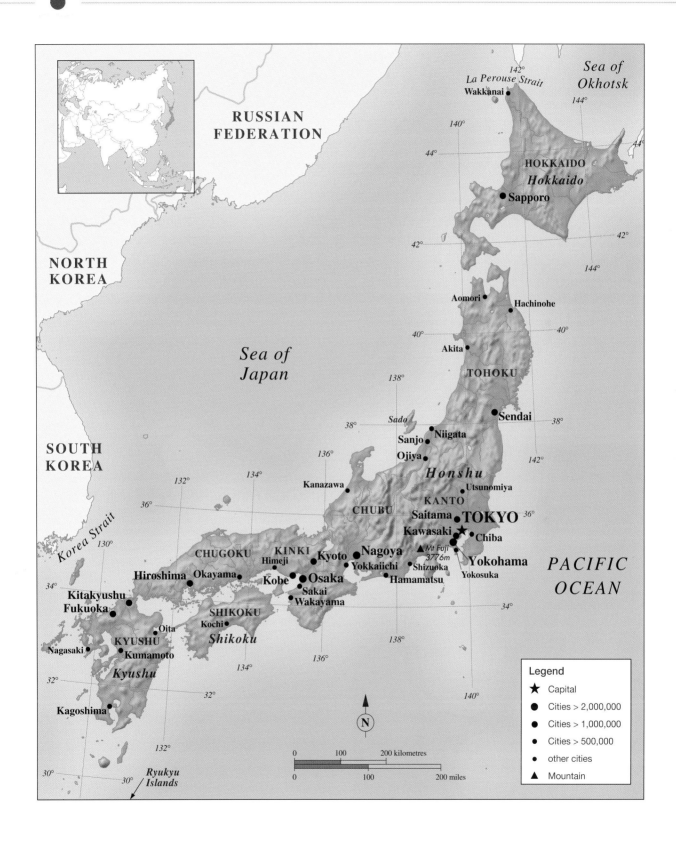

Sea of
Okhotsk

La Perouse Strait

RUSSIAN
FEDERATION

Wakkanai

HOKKAIDO
Hokkaido

Sapporo

NORTH
KOREA

Aomori   Hachinohe

Akita

TOHOKU

Sea of
Japan

Sado   Sendai

SOUTH
KOREA

Sanjo   Niigata
Ojiya

Honshu

Kanazawa

Utsunomiya

Korea Strait

CHUBU

KANTO
Saitama   **TOKYO**
Kawasaki   Chiba

CHUGOKU

KINKI
Himeji   Kyoto   Nagoya   ▲Mt Fuji
3776m   **Yokohama**
Yokkaiichi   Shizuoka
Hiroshima   Okayama   Kobe   Osaka   Hamamatsu   Yokosuka   PACIFIC
Sakai   OCEAN
Kitakyushu   Wakayama
Fukuoka   SHIKOKU
Oita   Kochi
KYUSHU   *Shikoku*
Nagasaki   Kumamoto
Kyushu

Kagoshima

*Ryukyu
Islands*

N

Legend	
★	Capital
●	Cities > 2,000,000
●	Cities > 1,000,000
•	Cities > 500,000
·	other cities
▲	Mountain

0   100   200 kilometres
0   100   200 miles

CHAPTER 2

History

Signs of early settlement in Japan can be traced back 30,000 years. Then, it is believed, Japan was joined to the Asian mainland by two land bridges, one to the north and one to the south. The earliest inhabitants probably migrated over these land bridges and were likely to have been hunter-gatherers who used stone tools and weapons. From around 10,000 BC, humans developed skills in pottery that allowed for improvements in the cooking and storing of food. The importance of this discovery is reflected in the fact that the era between 10,000 BC and 300 BC is known as the Jomon period, after the style of decoration on pottery made during that time.

CHINESE INFLUENCES

From 300 BC to 300 AD, during the period known as Yayoi, Japan was heavily influenced by ideas brought by migrants from China. These included the growing of rice as a staple crop, the working of iron and the weaving of cloth. Between the fourth and the seventh centuries, contact with China increased further and Japan adopted many aspects of Chinese culture including its writing system and calendar. Chinese technologies, such as the manufacture of porcelain, silk and paper were also introduced. The Buddhist religion also came to Japan from China. Buddhism fitted well with the existing Shinto religion, because it offered teachings on death while Shinto focused on life in this world.

SHOGUNS AND FEUDAL RULE

By the seventh century, Japan was ruled as an empire, although some historians think that Japan's line of emperors can be traced back to

? *Did you know?*

The *Ainu* were one of the earliest peoples to inhabit Japan. They are believed to have come originally from Siberia, as they share some skeletal characteristics with peoples from this area. On Hokkaido island there are still some *Ainu* who speak a language quite different from Japanese.

◀ Calligraphy, known as 'sho', was brought to Japan in the seventh century by Buddhist monks who used Chinese calligraphy in their scriptures.

400 AD, when a powerful family, the Fugiwara clan, controlled central Honshu. From the seventh to the eleventh centuries, the imperial court of the emperor was at its peak of power and influence in terms of the size of the territory it covered. The emperor had absolute power and was considered to be divinely appointed as a living god. This period is named the Heian (meaning 'peace' in Japanese) era and was noted for its art, poetry and literature. However, by the end of the era, in the twelfth century, military leaders (shoguns) had become very powerful. In 1192, Minamoto Yoritomo became the first shogun to seize control of government from the imperial court. There followed several centuries dominated by military rule, with leaders of different powerful families often battling for succession to title of shogun.

The Edo era (1600-1868) was dominated by the last shogun family – the Tokugawa clan. In 1603, the Tokugawa leader, Ieyasu, emerged as the most powerful feudal lord. He built a new capital at Edo (present day Tokyo). Everyday life for most Japanese people was grim, tightly controlled through a rigid feudal system in which a strict social hierarchy was imposed, with the shogun at the top, followed by the samurai and commoners.

▲ An illustration from 1865 shows soldiers forcing commoners to kneel before the shogun as he approaches on a journey from Edo (now Tokyo) to Kyoto to meet with the emperor.

Focus on: The seclusion of Japan in the Edo era

The isolationist policies of this era included banning Christianity, expelling foreigners and ending almost all overseas trade. Japanese people were also forbidden to leave the islands of Japan. For commercial reasons, people from China and the Dutch East India Company were allowed to visit Japan, but they were restricted to Dejima island near the port of Nagasaki. Any foreigners landing elsewhere in Japan were sentenced to death. Only after 1853 were foreign relations re-established when an American fleet, led by Commodore Perry, sailed to Japan and demanded it 'open up' to trade. In economic terms, many in Japan benefitted from this 'opening up', but the shogun rulers of the time were weakened by the episode and their reign ended relatively soon after, in 1868.

The Edo era saw the development of cultural rituals, some of which, like the Japanese tea ceremony (see page 49) or flower arranging, still exist today. The rituals were elaborate and expensive, so took up time and money which might otherwise have been used to mount a rebellion against the rulers. The rituals therefore helped the Tokugawa family control the other clans. In 1639, Japan was cut off from external influences when isolationist policies were imposed by a later Tokugawa shogun – Iemitsu.

MODERNIZATION, IMPERIALISM AND WAR

Between 1868 and 1912, the Meiji era (Meiji means 'enlightened rule') saw the resignation of the last Tokugawa shogun, Yoshinobu.

▼ The Meiji shrine in Tokyo was built in memory of Emperor Meiji and Empress Shoken and completed in 1920.

Following the Boshin War (1868-9) between Yoshinobu and pro-imperial forces, the emperor was re-established as ruler, and Japan became known as the Empire of Japan. The emperor continued to be advised by leaders of the pro-imperial forces, such as Okubo Toshimichi and Saigo Takamori, who had a great influence on how Japan was governed. They were behind decisions such as the lifting of restrictions on contact with foreign

Did you know?

During the rule of the shoguns, the samurai, the warriors of the lords, were the only people, apart from the shoguns, who could be armed. The samurai had the legal right to kill any commoner (for example, peasants, artisans, merchants, outcasts and others in the social classes below them) who did not show respect for their feudal lord.

influences, which allowed trade with Europe and China to develop again. Japan began to modernize, bringing in foreign experts to teach in specialist fields such as engineering and science. Feudalism was abolished and the principle of democratic government was established, although only wealthy men over the age of 25 were allowed to vote.

Japan needed raw materials to fuel its rapid industrialization so it set out to annex neighbouring territories. The first Chinese-Japanese War of 1894-95 was fought in Korea, and led to Japan's annexation of Taiwan (then called Formosa). The Russo-Japanese War of 1904-5 was fought in Manchuria and led to Japan's annexation of Korea.

During the First World War (1914-18), Japan fought on the side of the Allies and emerged in 1919 as a major world power, with increased influence in Asia. After the war, a democratic system of government was re-established. However, during the early 1920s economic problems, made worse in the Tokyo area by the devastation caused by the Great Kanto earthquake in 1923, led to a rise in the influence of military leaders. Extreme nationalism, focusing on the preservation of traditional Japanese values and the rejection of Western influence, took hold and became increasingly powerful. In 1931, nationalist extremists assassinated the Japanese prime minister, Hamaguchi Osachi, and military leaders gained influence. Japan undertook military action to expand its territory. Japanese forces invaded Manchuria in 1931 and then, in 1937, launched into a second major war against China. This developed into the Pacific War and became part of the Second World War (1939-45). The Imperial Japanese Army carried out widespread atrocities during the war with China, including the Massacre of Nanjing in 1937, in which over 300,000 unarmed civilians of the city of Nanjing are alleged to have been killed.

▲ Osaka castle is one of several fine castles in Japan. It was first completed in 1583, but has been rebuilt several times since, most recently in 1931.

DEFEAT AND OCCUPATION

In 1940, the fall of France to Japan's ally, Germany, led to the Japanese occupation of French Indo-China. In 1941, Japan launched a surprise attack on the US naval base at Pearl Harbor in which more than 2,500 US sailors were killed. The USA responded by declaring war on Japan. In 1942, Japan seized control of Singapore. But Japanese military defeats by the Allies followed and, in August 1945, the dropping of two US atomic bombs on the cities of Hiroshima and Nagasaki forced Japan's rapid surrender. Following the Second World War the Allies imposed a new constitution on Japan, and US forces occupied the country for the next seven years. After occupation ended, Japan signed an alliance with the USA that has been maintained in various forms to this day. Japan regained political independence in 1952, although the USA retained the Okinawa islands for military use. In 1972, the islands were politically transferred back to Japan, although US forces still have a presence there.

▼ This building in Hiroshima was one of the few left standing following the dropping of the atomic bomb in 1945. Now known as the A-bomb Dome, it is a permanent memorial to those who died.

 Did you know?

On 9 March 1945, in just one night of firebombing by the US military, more than 100,000 Japanese, most of them civilians, were killed in Tokyo. Six hundred bombers dropped more than 500,000 incendiary bombs. Over 41 sq km (16 sq miles) of the city were completely destroyed.

Focus on: The atomic bombs of 1945

On 6 August 1945, an American B29 bomber dropped a uranium atomic bomb on the city of Hiroshima. Three days later, a second atomic bomb, this time using plutonium, was dropped on the city of Nagasaki. By the end of 1945, more than 200,000 Japanese had died from these bombs. This total does not include the thousands of Koreans who were working as slave labourers in factories in the two cities. In the years immediately following the explosions, nothing was known in Japan about the nuclear fallout and radiation sickness that went on to kill thousands more. Sixty years after the bombings, people are still dying from cancers caused by nuclear radiation.

Japan still has an emperor on the Chrysanthemum Throne (see page 25), the oldest hereditary monarchy in the world. But the emperor has had no ruling powers or influence on the elected government since the end of the Second World War.

RECOVERY AND GROWTH

During the 1960s and 1970s, rapid growth returned Japan to economic strength, and it became the world's leading manufacturer of ships and steel. During the 1970s, oil crises caused the Japanese government to rethink its whole economy. Japan's heavy industries used large quantities of oil (of which Japan had none of its own supplies). This meant that Japan was dependent on other countries for vital supplies of energy. To relieve this, Japan began a nuclear energy programme and started to switch from heavy industries to higher value and high-tech industries producing goods such as cameras and electrical items. Japan soon became famous worldwide for efficiency and advanced technology. However, this came at a huge cost to the environment as industrial processes caused serious pollution and natural habitats were destroyed.

INTO THE TWENTY-FIRST CENTURY

In the 1990s Japan faced growing economic competition from the 'Asian Tigers'. This slump in economic growth has become known as Japan's 'lost decade'. The twenty-first century has seen improvements in the economy and some significant political changes. The dominant political party, the Liberal Democrat Party (LDP), suffered a temporary loss of power in 1993, as a result of political scandals and corruption involving some of its politicians. Eventually the LDP

▲ A production line making Sony Triniton televisions in 1973. The manufacture of electronic goods was a major factor in Japan's economic recovery during the 1960s and 1970s.

regained power in 2000. Its popularity increased again following the election of Prime Minister Junichiro Koizumi in 2001. Koizumi's flamboyant personality makes him popular with the people, as do his assurances that he will deal with economic problems and corruption. Koizumi has spearheaded considerable developments in Japan's foreign policy. For example, in 2002 he became the first Japanese prime minister to visit the communist state of North Korea.

CHAPTER 3

Landscape and Climate

Japan is made up of about 6,800 islands that form a crescent-shaped archipelago lying north to south. It stretches over more than 20 degrees of latitude, is located in the Pacific Ocean, and is separated from the east coast of Asia by the Sea of Japan. Japan's nearest neighbours are Russia (to the north-west), North and South Korea (to the west) and China (to the south-west). The nearest country on the Asian mainland is South Korea, at a distance of approximately 200 km (124 miles) over the Korea Strait.

MOUNTAINS, RIVERS, LAKES AND COASTS

While Mount Fuji is Japan's highest mountain, there are fourteen other peaks over 3,000 m (9,843 ft). Most are extinct or dormant volcanoes and are part of the Japanese Alps that run through central Honshu. The low-lying areas of Japan are broken

▼ The coastline near Kagoshima on Kyushu is very rocky. These formations were the result of volcanic activity, which forced molten lava up through the sea.

up into many small plains, separated from one another by high ground. The largest lowland area is the Kanto Plain on Honshu. It is about 13,000 sq km (5,019 sq miles) in area, and is where Japan's largest urban concentration, including the city of Tokyo, is located.

Japan's rivers drain either to the east into the Pacific Ocean or to the west into the Sea of Japan between Japan and Korea. Rivers are very short, as nowhere in Japan is far from the sea. The longest river is the Shinano, flowing over a distance of 367 km (228 miles) through the Nagano and Niigata prefectures into the Sea of Japan. Rivers in the mountains are fast-flowing and provide some potential for the generation of hydro-electric power (HEP). At certain times of the year, when rainfall or snowfall is high, there is a significant risk of flooding in the lower reaches of these rivers. To reduce this risk, concrete channels have been built to funnel water quickly and efficiently to the sea.

There are many lakes in Japan's uplands, often in the craters of old volcanoes. The largest of these is Lake Biwa, measuring 670 sq km (259 sq miles). The next in size is Lake Kasumi, measuring only 168 sq km (65 sq miles). Lake Biwa is famous for its beauty and is a popular place for leisure pursuits. During the 1980s it became polluted with sewage and urban waste, but it was cleaned up in the late 1990s.

As an archipelago, Japan has a very long coastline of 29,751 km (18,475 miles). The Pacific coastline to the south of Tokyo has many long, narrow and relatively shallow inlets that provide natural harbours. The Inland Sea separates the islands of Shikoku, Honshu and Kyushu.

▲ Lake Mashu in Akan national park, Hokkaido, is often called Japan's most beautiful lake. Its waters are clear to a depth of up to 35 m (115 ft).

▲ A man pushes his bicycle past one of the many thousands of homes destroyed in the Kobe earthquake of 1995 that killed more than 6,000 people in Japan.

VOLCANOES AND EARTHQUAKES

Japan is located on a very unstable part of the earth's crust where three tectonic plates – the Pacific, Philippine and Eurasian – meet. Movement of the plates causes volcanoes and earthquakes. As a consequence of its location, Japan has about 10 per cent of the world's active volcanoes. Volcanoes that have erupted in the last ten years include Tokachi on Hokkaido, Aso on Kyushu and Asama, Honshu's most active volcano, located 140 km (87 miles) north-west of Tokyo.

Earthquakes are frequent, with as many as 1,500 recorded per year. Most of these are minor tremors. Major earthquakes that cause considerable damage and loss of life are very infrequent. In October 2004, an earthquake measuring 6.2 on the Richter scale struck the town of Ojiya and its surrounding area in the Niigata prefecture. More than twenty people were killed, 1,800 were injured and 60,000 were evacuated from their homes. Earthquakes of this scale often cause other hazards such as landslides and tsunamis.

 Did you know?

Although Mount Fuji is now dormant, it used to be an active volcano. Between the years of 781 and 1707, it erupted at least sixteen times. It has not erupted since 1707.

EFFECTS OF LATITUDE

Japan lies almost directly north to south, which means that latitude is a major influence on climate. For example Hokkaido, to the north, has cool summers and long, cold winters where average temperatures often fall below freezing. By contrast, Kyushu to the south, has a humid, subtropical climate with winter temperatures generally above 10°C (50°F). Japan also experiences seasonal variations, particularly in relation to precipitation. The average annual amount is about 2,000 mm (79 in) and approximately 75 per cent of this falls between June and October. This is because during this period the prevailing winds blow in from the warm Pacific Ocean and are laden with moisture. These conditions can create typhoons that bring torrential rain and strong winds, causing damage and disruption. In the winter months, prevailing winds from the Asian landmass often bring heavy snow to the north and north-west of Japan. The snow blocks roads and causes flooding when it melts.

▼ Residents rescue possessions from flooded houses in Sanjo, about 300 km (186 miles) north of Tokyo following a typhoon in July 2004 that caused widespread damage.

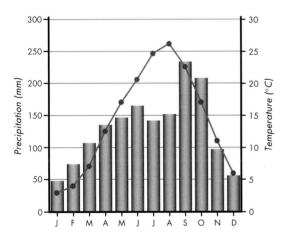

▲ Average monthly climate conditions in Tokyo

Focus on: Typhoons

Japan lies in the path of severe storms that originate in tropical areas of the Pacific Ocean where sea temperatures are above 27°C (81°F). These storms, known as typhoons in this part of the world (and as hurricanes in the Atlantic/Caribbean) occur between the months of July and October when sea temperatures are high. Typhoons with winds of between 74-155 mph (125-249 kmph) and torrential rain may cause loss of life and great damage. In October 2004, more than seventy people died, hillsides were washed away and trees were uprooted during Typhoon Tokage, the most destructive typhoon to hit Japan for twenty-five years.

CHAPTER 4

Population and Settlements

The population of Japan is about 127.8 million. Until the mid-1980s, the Japanese population experienced significant growth, rising from 99 million in 1965 to 121 million in 1985. Since then this growth has slowed, and the birth rate has fallen from 1,948 per 1,000 in 1975 to 1,139 per 1,000 in 2003. Current projections indicate that the population will fall to about 124 million by 2020. One reason for this is the age at which Japanese men and women now marry. This has risen from 28.9 years for men and 24.2 years for women in 1970, to 29.4 and 27.6 respectively in 2003. It seems that women are delaying getting married because it often means they can no longer work outside the home. In traditional Japanese culture, married women are seen as home-makers.

LIFE EXPECTANCY

As the birth rate has fallen, life expectancy has increased, from 73 years in 1975 to 83 years in 2003. This combination of trends is leading to an ageing of the population. The proportion of those over the age of 65 has increased from 8 per cent of the population in 1975 to 19 per cent in 2003, while the proportion of those under the age of 15 has fallen from 25 per cent to 14 per cent over the same period. By 2020, the proportion of those over age 65 is expected to be around 27 per cent.

These trends, common to many economically developed countries, are viewed with concern by the Japanese government. It fears that a growing proportion of older people will put a strain on health and pension services. But there is a more positive view which suggests that, in wealthy countries such as Japan, people remain youthful because of healthy lifestyles and higher quality healthcare. They therefore have the potential to earn their own living for much longer than in the past. Japan already has a tradition of people (although usually only men) staying economically active into their 70s and 80s.

◀ Kogan-ji temple in Sugamo, Tokyo, is popular with older people. They believe that if they douse a small statue called 'Migawari Kannon' with water it will take away their aches, pains and other medical problems.

ETHNIC ORIGINS

Over 98 per cent of the population is ethnically Japanese, making it one of the most homogenous countries in the world. This is partly because Japan's island nature means that there has been little migration to it. In the early twentieth century, however, Japan's occupation of Korea and Taiwan resulted in people from these countries migrating to work in Japan's coal mines. Today, approximately 0.6 per cent of the population is Korean, and many of these people are descendants of the earlier miners (Japanese citizenship is based on nationality of parents, not place of birth.)

Two other groups are identified as different from mainstream Japanese society. The first is the *Ainu* (see page 8), an indigenous minority group with a distinctive culture. The present-day *Ainu* are descended from hunter-gatherers who settled in the northern Japanese islands before 300 BC. The *Ainu* are dwindling in numbers and are now only to be found living in Hokkaido. They have suffered from discrimination in the past, and although there is now greater recognition of their rights and culture, they are often seen by mainstream Japanese society only as a tourist attraction. The second distinct group that faces discrimination in Japan is the *buraku* people (see page 21).

Did you know?

It is rare in Japan for unmarried couples to have children. The delay in getting married means that the age at which a woman has her first child has risen, from 25.6 years in 1970, to 28.6 in 2003.

▲ A busy pedestrian crossing in Osaka city centre. Japan has a large population, but one that is overwhelmingly from a single ethnic group.

Population data

- Population: 127.8 million
- Population 0-14 yrs: 14%
- Population 15-64 yrs: 67%
- Population 65+ yrs: 19%
- Population growth rate: 0.1%
- Population density: 341.0 per sq km/ 883.3 per sq mile
- Urban population: 65%
- Major cities: Tokyo 35,327,000
    Osaka 11,286,000
    Nagoya 3,189,000

Source: United Nations and World Bank

WHERE PEOPLE LIVE

The Japanese population is very unevenly distributed because of the limited amount of flat low land suitable for settlements and the fast rate at which urbanization has taken place. The average population density for Japan as a whole is 341 per sq km (883.3 per sq mile). Some regions are sparsely populated; for example, Hokkaido has 73 people per sq km (189 per sq mile). But some Tokyo districts have over 11,000 people per sq km (28,490 per sq mile), one of the highest population densities in the world.

▲ This level land around Lake Biwa is densely settled in what is otherwise a mountainous terrain. Level land is at a premium in Japan.

Approximately 65 per cent of people live in urban areas. The rate of urbanization has been very high during the past fifty years, with rural areas losing people to the fast-growing towns and cities. Since the 1970s, however, much of Japan's urban growth has come from an internal population increase, and small town and rural populations have stabilized. There are twelve cities with more than one million people, and all except one (Sapporo) are located in the Pacific Belt on the Kanto Plain, Honshu. At the eastern end of the Pacific Belt, four major cities – Tokyo, Yokohama, Kawasaki and Chiba – have spread and joined up to make one huge metropolitan area containing 35 million people.

INSIDE CITIES

Japanese cities do not have the rich and poor districts or neighbourhoods commonly found in US or UK cities, where the poor tend to live in run-down inner city areas with social problems, and the wealthy are found in well-maintained, orderly suburban locations. It is often thought that this is because Japanese society is more equal than elsewhere. Although Japan does have less of a gap between the incomes of rich and poor than either the UK or the USA, significant differences still exist between households. These differences are reflected in income, job status and quality of housing. However, 'well-off' and 'less well-off' households are not generally concentrated in particular areas of the cities (though there are

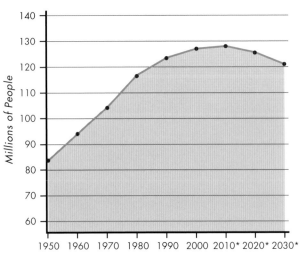

* Projected Population

▲ Population growth 1950-2030

exceptions – see Focus box below). The reason for this is partly because Japanese employers usually pay the transport costs of their employees, so poorer people can live in the suburbs and commute to work. Also, wealthy residents do not need to express their social status according to where they live. This is because, in Japan, people who want to impress friends or work colleagues tend to wine and dine them in restaurants rather than entertain them at home.

▲ In Japan's main cities, high density housing is the only practical and affordable option when space is so limited.

Focus on: The *buraku* people

Although ethnically identical to other Japanese, the *buraku* people, or *burakumin*, are discriminated against because they are descendants of an outcast class that existed in the feudal system of the seventeenth century. At this time the *burakumin* were at the bottom of a rigid hierarchy, doing jobs that were associated with the impurities of death (burials, for example). Within the Buddhist and Shinto religions they were thought to be polluted. This caste system was abolished in 1871 and today the *burakumin* no longer have to wear special clothes and live separately. Some, however, still live in *burakumin* communities that are generally 'looked down upon' by the wider society. They still face discrimination, particularly when they wish to marry or apply for a job. Potential marriage partners or employers can find out the details of an individual's origins through Japan's family registry system. If the person's origins are *burakumin*, there is a strong possibility that he or she will be rejected. This discrimination leads to unhappiness and economic problems. A recent survey by the Buraku Liberation League (BLL), an organization that fights for *burakumin* rights, showed that unemployment figures in *burakumin* communities, such as Kuboyoshi district of Osaka, were twice the national average. There are more than 4,000 *burakumin* communities, with an official population total of 892,000. However the BLL believes the total is higher, at around three million, because many do not admit publicly to being *burakumin*.

CHAPTER 5

Government and Politics

Japan has a democratic parliamentary government that is based on a constitution. Parliament is made up of the House of Representatives and the House of Councillors, known jointly as the Diet. All Japanese nationals over the age of 20, regardless of gender or ethnic origins, are able to vote for members of the Diet. These members elect the prime minister, who is the head of government. The prime minister is usually the leader of the largest political party represented in the Diet.

▼ The National Diet Building in Tokyo is the seat of the Japanese government. It was built between 1920 and 1936 and is at the centre of a district of government buildings located behind the Imperial Palace.

THE LIBERAL DEMOCRATIC PARTY

Since the 1950s, one party, the Liberal Democratic Party, has dominated the political scene. In 1993, the LDP fell from power for the first time in twenty years as a result of political scandals and corruption. Some LDP politicians were accused of 'buying' support by setting up large schemes, for example, building roads that were not needed but which provided construction jobs. These schemes were financed by public money from sources such as the savings bank, run by the state-owned postal system, Japan Post. Nevertheless, the lack of a strong opposition party has led to the LDP's recovery in recent years and, in 2000, it became the ruling party again. Since

then, support for the LDP has varied. It only held on to power in the 2003 election by virtue of a coalition with two minor parties, but it won the 2005 election with the biggest majority since the 1980s.

THE JAPANESE MONARCHY

Japan has the world's oldest hereditary monarchy, headed by an emperor and known as the Chrysanthemum Throne (see page 25). Until the Second World War, the emperor had the status of a living god, but this was changed with the imposition of a constitution by the Allied forces immediately after the war. Today the emperor has no political power, but answers to the elected government.

THE CONSTITUTION AND FOREIGN POLICY

Japan's present constitution dates from 1947 and provides the foundation for a democratic, peaceful nation. Article 9 of the constitution renounces the use of force to settle international disputes. Until 2003, Japan's foreign policy was strongly pacifist, in line with its constitution. Since the Second World War, Japan has had Self Defence Forces (SDF) instead of militaristic armed forces. The SDF have been concerned only with defending Japan from a direct attack. In 1992, a law was passed allowing the SDF to venture abroad as long as they were part of a United Nations (UN) mission and that a ceasefire was in place. This enabled Japan to contribute to peace-keeping in a number of countries, including Cambodia in 1992, Mozambique in 1993 and East Timor in 2002. However, in 2003, Prime Minister Koizumi proposed an emergency law to allow the SDF to be sent to Iraq, to show support for the USA. The troops were to be sent in a humanitarian rather than aggressive

role, to support reconstruction efforts, but there was concern among opposition politicians and the public that Japan was moving away from its pacifist principles. The law was passed and, in 2004, for the first time since the Second World War, Japanese troops were sent to a combat zone to carry out their humanitarian role.

▲ The Japanese prime minister, Junichiro Koizumi (on the right) at a campaign rally during the 2003 election.

 Did you know?

Although they have been able to vote since 1947, there are very few women in positions of power in the government. In 2004, women made up only 9.7 per cent of members of the Diet (the national parliament). A government strategy know as the Plan for Gender Equality 2000 has set a target of 30 per cent for 2007, but progress towards this is slow.

There have been other pressures on Japan to reconsider its pacifist stance. For example, there are potential threats from neighbouring North Korea (see page 36) and there has been an increase in international security issues related to terrorism.

INTERNATIONAL RELATIONS

Japan's relations with the neighbouring countries of China, Russia, South Korea and North Korea are very complex. Japan recognizes the need for co-operation between them, not least because of the high degree of economic interdependence that exists in the region. This has become increasingly important in the past ten years, as the economies of China and South Korea have grown stronger. However, Japan's standing in the region is considerably hampered by legacies from the Second World War. Japan has made statements apologizing for its war-time atrocities, but various present-day incidents continue to cause tension. For example, in 2005, Prime Minister Koizumi insisted on carrying out formal visits to the Yasukuni war memorial (he had visited it every year since he was first elected in 2001). This memorial honours some of Japan's military leaders of the past, including those convicted as war criminals for crimes against Chinese and Korean citizens. China and South Korea strongly resented this, not least because they feared that Koizumi might favour a return to Japan's more militaristic past.

▼ The controversial Yasukuni war memorial is at the centre of tense diplomatic relations between Japan and its neighbours in China and South Korea.

Since the end of the Second World War, Japan has maintained a significant and generally positive relationship with the USA. From the end of the war until 1952, the USA occupied Japan. In 1960, the US-Japan Security Treaty was signed in which it was agreed that the US would provide Japan with a nuclear shield. This meant that US military vessels, equipped with nuclear weapons and patrolling through Japanese waters, would respond to a military attack on Japan. This agreement continues today, providing the USA with an essential strategic base in the Pacific, while Japan benefits from US protection. In recent years there has been some debate among Japanese politicians about whether Japan should now take responsibility for its own defence and not be so closely tied to the USA.

Did you know?

Japan has ongoing territorial disputes, over several different groups of islands, with all its neighbouring countries. For example, Japan refuses to accept that the Southern Kuril Islands (known as the 'northern territories' in Japan) are part of Russia, as was claimed by Russia at the end of the Second World War. As a result, Russia and Japan have still not signed a post-war peace treaty.

Focus on: The future of the Chrysanthemum Throne

The Chrysanthemum Throne is so-called because this flower features in the coat of arms of the Imperial Household; it is the world's oldest hereditary monarchy and has existed for over 2,600 years. Until the Second World War, this imperial dynasty ruled over Japan, but was replaced by a democratic government in 1947. Since then, the Imperial Household, headed by the emperor, performs only ceremonial and social duties. The 1889 Imperial House Law regulates succession and forbids women ascending to the throne. By 2005, no boys had been born into the family for nearly forty years. The immediate heir to the throne, Prince Naruhito, has a daughter, born in 2001. Concern over continuation of the imperial line, unbroken for 125 generations, prompted Prime Minister Koizumi to set up a special commission of legal experts to discuss whether to reform the law in 2006. There have been eight empresses in the past (the last one was in the 1700s). Empresses have only reigned temporarily, until a male heir has grown old enough to take over. According to a recent opinion poll it seems that the Japanese may be ready to accept a change, with 80 per cent of people happy for a woman to take the throne.

▲ Nijubashi bridge and a seventeenth-century guard tower form part of the Imperial Palace compound in central Tokyo.

CHAPTER 6

Energy and Resources

Japan is very short of domestic energy resources, with limited oil and natural gas reserves. As Japan is the fourth largest energy consumer in the world – after the USA, China and Russia – this means that energy resources must be imported to meet the demand. Japan is the world's second largest energy importer, after the USA. Until 1973, Japan relied on cheap oil imports from the Middle East. However, Japan was forced to rethink its energy policy following oil crises in 1973 and 1979 when oil became far more expensive. Japan adopted several strategies to reduce its dependence on oil, including the promotion of energy saving measures and the development of alternative sources such as nuclear energy, natural gas and renewable energies.

Oil is still imported from many different countries, including the United Arab Emirates and Saudi Arabia, but it now accounts for less than 50 per cent of primary energy requirements compared with 75 per cent in the early 1970s. Coal used to be mined in Japan, but the last mine closed in 2002 because it cost more to mine coal than to buy it from abroad. Coal still contributes 19 per cent of the primary energy requirements, but now Japan imports it from Australia, China and Sakhalin (a Russian island to the north of Hokkaido). Oil and gas reserves in Sakhalin may well provide Japan with significant supplies in future. Natural gas is imported from Brunei and Indonesia, and provides a further 13 per cent of the country's fuel.

DOMESTIC ENERGY SOURCES

Japan has developed nuclear energy in an attempt to reduce energy imports. Although the uranium needed for this needs to be imported, the amount required is relatively small. Also, the countries from which it is bought, mainly Australia and Canada, are politically stable, which means that the supply of uranium is unlikely to be disrupted by political crises.

◀ Japan is an energy hungry economy, as clearly illustrated here by a brightly lit Tokyo skyline.

With fifty-one power stations in operation, Japan has the third biggest nuclear energy programme in the world, after the USA and France. Approximately 26.9 per cent of Japan's electricity is generated by nuclear power, compared with 62 per cent generated from fossil fuels. Government plans to expand the nuclear contribution by 30 per cent by 2010 will require the construction of twelve more reactors. However, there are growing concerns from the Japanese public about the safety of nuclear power.

▲ A power station located in Tokyo's main harbour uses imported oil as a fuel to generate electricity.

Other 0.4%
Renewables 2.3%
HEP 8.4%
Nuclear 26.9%
Oil 13.2%
Gas 22.3%
Coal 26.5%

▲ Electricity production by type

Focus on: The nuclear energy dilemma

Despite the significant part that nuclear power has played in tackling the problem of dependence on imported oil, Japan's nuclear industry faces an uncertain future. The confidence of the Japanese public has been shaken by a series of incidents that have raised concerns about the safety of nuclear power. In 2002, seventeen reactors were shut down when it was discovered that they had not been maintained in line with government regulations. It took two years before they were fully re-opened again, after full checks had been carried out. Then, in 2004, an accident at another reactor claimed the lives of four workers. Those who support nuclear energy argue that this loss of life is no greater than that which results from accidents in other industries. But the 2004 accident, combined with more general fears about the safe disposal of nuclear waste, has increased public opposition to nuclear energy. The Japanese government is attempting to rebuild public confidence in the nuclear option by stressing the role it can play in reducing greenhouse gas emissions. The government will need to win back public support if it hopes to press ahead with its planned expansion of nuclear energy.

The Japanese government is carrying out research into alternative sources of energy as part of the policy to tackle the dependence on imported energy and nuclear power. Although there are many mountain rivers with rapid flow, they are generally too small for large-scale commercial development of hydro-electric power (HEP). At present, HEP is used to generate 8.4 per cent of Japan's electricity and there is little scope to expand beyond this. Other sources being investigated are wind, solar, wave and geothermal power.

Energy data

- Energy consumption as % of world total: 5.1%
- Energy consumption by sector (% of total):
  Industry: 44
  Transportation: 27
  Agriculture: 3
  Services: 12
  Residential: 14
- CO_2 emissions as % of world total: 5
- CO_2 emissions per capita in tonnes p.a.: 9.1

Source: World Resources Institute

RESOURCES FROM LAND AND SEA

Japan lacks mineral resources such as iron ore, copper and bauxite. These are particularly important to industry and therefore they have to be imported. Gold, magnesium and silver have been found in Japan in sufficient amounts to meet the needs of domestic industries. With over 66 per cent of Japan's land area covered by forests, timber is an important domestic resource. But there are often high costs involved in exploiting it, because steep slopes and lack of roads makes access to the

▼ Malaysian timber being handled by a Japanese cargo vessel in Minimata Bay, Kyushu. The majority of Japan's timber needs are imported.

forested areas difficult. It is generally cheaper to import timber and, in 2002, over 80 per cent of timber needs were met this way. Japan is the world's largest importer of tropical timber. Environmental groups and local communities in countries such as Cameroon and Papua New Guinea have criticized Japanese companies for the extensive felling of tropical rainforests in these countries.

Historically, fishing has been an essential industry for Japan as an island nation, and has provided both employment and an important source of food for the population. The Pacific Ocean off Japan's east coast, where two currents meet, has provided rich fishing grounds. However, since the late 1980s the catch has declined from over 12 million tonnes (11,810,478 tons) in 1989 to just under 6 million tonnes (5,905,239 tons) in 2002. This decline is the result of overfishing and of the drop in numbers of people employed in fishing. In 1953, the workforce was 800,000, but by 2003 this had fallen to 238,000. Younger workers are not replacing older ones when they retire, and currently over 34 per cent of those people who fish commercially are over the age of 65.

Annual consumption of fish remains relatively high at over 11 million tonnes (10.83 tons) in 2002, with 75 kg (165 lb) eaten per head of population compared with the world average of 16 kg (35 lb). To meet this demand, Japan's imports of fish have risen five-fold over the last twenty years. The increase in imports, from countries such as China, the USA, Thailand, Indonesia and Russia, is partly explained by a greater demand for more luxury types of fish, such as tuna and salmon (rather than mackerel and pollack), which cannot be met from local waters.

▼ Tsukiji fish market in Tokyo is one of the largest in the world and is a showcase for Japan's long history of using the sea as a resource.

CHAPTER 7

Economy and Income

Japan's economy is made up of two distinct tiers. The first consists of a small number of large and highly efficient manufacturing companies geared to producing goods for export, such as cars and household electrical goods. Many have become globally known brand names, such as Toyota and Sony. Nippon Steel, although not so well-known outside Japan, is equally important and is the world's second biggest steel producer (after Arcelor of Luxembourg). The second tier consists of numerous small to medium sized companies, often family-owned, which produce items for the domestic market or components for the export companies. For example, Morino Industries, based near Tokyo, employs thirty-seven people and makes metal frames for the manufacturers of wide-screen televisions. About 99 per cent of Japan's manufacturing concerns are smaller companies with 300 or fewer employees.

JAPAN AS A WORLD ECONOMIC POWER

Japan has the world's second largest economy (after the USA). Japan achieved this status during the 1960s and early 1970s, when it had the world's highest economic growth rates of around 11 per cent a year. This was mainly brought about by the tier of large, highly efficient companies mass-producing consumer goods primarily for the US market. Exports from these companies earned the foreign revenue needed to buy the raw materials that Japan lacked, particularly oil and iron ore. High-tech industries were particularly suited to Japan, as they needed only small amounts of raw materials and energy, and depended upon the skilled and well-educated workforce that Japan had developed since the Second World War. Japan's economic growth was particularly remarkable given the widespread destruction of its industries that had taken place during the war, and led some observers to refer to this period as Japan's 'economic miracle'.

▲ A shipyard in Kobe: shipbuilding is one of Japan's most important heavy industries, producing ships for both domestic and international markets.

Economic data

- Gross National Income (GNI) in US$: 4,749,910,000,000
- World rank by GNI: 2
- GNI per capita in US$: 37,810
- World rank by GNI per capita: 9
- Economic growth: 2.7%

Source: World Bank

As with other wealthy nations, Japan's economic development has been in the manufacturing and services sectors, both of which tend to be urban based. The rural economies of agriculture and forestry have shrunk, with employment in the industries that produce and provide raw materials dropping from 37 per cent of the labour force in 1975 to 4.6 per cent in 2003. Agricultural land is very productive, with the crop yields per hectare among the highest in the world. However, only about 15 per cent of the land area is suitable for farming and much of this is too expensive to be used for agriculture. There has been a significant decline in the amount of food that Japan grows for itself, as it is cheaper to import food from the USA and China. In 2003, Japan met only about 40 per cent of its food needs, compared with 75 per cent in 1965.

RECESSION AND ITS AFTERMATH

During the 1990s, the previously impressive growth rates slowed dramatically. The economy grew at only 1 per cent or less per year. This recession was partly triggered by changes in the exchange rate system that existed between Japan and the USA. In 1985, the Plaza Accord devalued the US dollar, changing its value in relation to the yen. Following the Accord, the US dollar was worth 120 yen, about one third of its value in 1970. Japanese export goods became more expensive and less competitive in the global market, and this led

 Did you know?

Despite the 'lost decade' Japan is still a major economic power in the world. In 2003, Japan's exports accounted for 5.9 per cent of the world trade in goods and services and for 5.23 per cent of global imports.

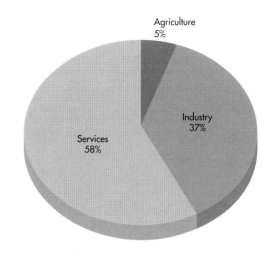

▲ Contribution by sector to national income

▲ The Roppongi Hills complex in Tokyo is a model for Japan's future, reviving part of the city into a modern business, retail and entertainment centre.

to Japanese companies shifting much of their production to countries with cheap labour rates, such as South-east Asia and China. For some time, Japanese companies were able to continue to sell their goods cheaply, but problems began to arise as the host countries themselves began to produce cheaper versions of high-tech goods.

By the early 1990s, Japan could not compete with these cheaper rivals. It was also heavily dependent on the global rather than the domestic market, partly because its manufacturing capacity had been much reduced. Since the end of the 1990s, the economic situation has shown signs of recovery as Japanese companies have started to develop strategies such as 'one of a kind'

▼ One way in which Japan has maintained its competitiveness is to set up overseas factories where labour costs are lower. This Sony television production line is in Vietnam.

production (see Focus box opposite) to deal with the challenges posed by the increased competition they face.

Japan's unemployment rate has traditionally been very low. For example, during the years of the economic miracle, the rate varied between 2.1 and 2.8 per cent. However, during the 1990s it rose to 5.6 per cent (although this was still well below that of many European Union countries, such as France with 8.9 per cent). The national figure is now 4.4 per cent, but there are variations between social groups (rates are higher for young people, with 9.3 per cent of those aged 15-24 out of work in 2004).

WOMEN IN THE WORKFORCE

Traditional attitudes about the role of women in Japanese society mean that, although women now make up about 40 per cent of the workforce, they still only fill about 9 per cent

of managerial posts. Also, they only get paid 59 per cent of men's wages. Measures to tackle such discrimination include the Equal Employment Opportunities Law for Men and Women, passed in 1986. But when jobs are few, for example, during a recession, women tend to lose out. The considerable cultural resistance towards women having careers means that the law tends to be ignored. However, there is a growing awareness in the wider society that more women will be needed in the future when the number of economically active people is likely to drop because of the ageing population.

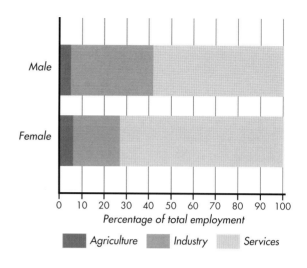

▲ Labour force by sector and gender

Focus on: Post-recession strategy of 'one of a kind' production

The 'lost decade' has prompted many of Japan's leading companies to develop strategies to tackle the competition they face. Japan's large electronics companies, such as Sharp, are developing 'one of a kind' products to compete with the low-cost mass produced goods in the factories of South Korea, Taiwan and China. They are searching for new technological niches for products that demand high-tech precision and advanced manufacturing techniques. For example, in 2005, Sharp announced the development of a split LCD screen for televisions that would allow two people to watch different programmes or use different functions (such as viewing TV and surfing the Internet) at the same time. The companies must keep their manufacturing techniques secret. This often means using them only in domestic factories, rather than overseas, where it may harder to

protect them from their rivals. Many companies are investing in research to develop these high quality niche products. For example, in 2005 Canon established a research centre near Tokyo and built a new factory for the manufacture of 'top of the range' digital cameras in Oita prefecture.

▶ Japanese industry is specializing in unique, high quality products. This robot suit has been developed by Professor Yoshiyuki Sankai to assist the elderly by giving them twice their usual strength.

CHAPTER 8

Global Connections

Many of Japan's leading companies, such as Toshiba and Canon, invest in other countries by setting up factories there. Or they may invest their money in an overseas company in return for a share in the profits and a degree of control over what the company does. Some companies, such as Honda, have cut transportation costs by moving closer to customer demand. For example, Honda has a large factory in Swindon, UK, which is an excellent location because it is close to numerous customers in the heavily populated south of England. By moving production to countries such as China, Taiwan and South Korea, Japanese companies have benefited from wage rates between twenty and thirty times lower than those in Japan. However, in the last decade, Japanese companies have found themselves in competition with the domestic companies of these countries. The domestic companies can produce the same goods as Japanese companies for an even cheaper price. The result is that some Japanese companies have cut back on their overseas low-cost production and are concentrating on high-tech precision manufacturing within Japan.

OVERSEAS DEVELOPMENT AID

In terms of overseas development aid (ODA), since the 1980s Japan has been one of the most generous countries in the world. ODA is given in various ways, including grants of money, technical help and loans. It is an important part of Japan's foreign policy, partly because it is often given with certain 'strings' attached. This means that the country receiving the ODA must usually, in return, allow Japan access to its natural resources. For example, Indonesia, which has received a lot of aid from Japan during the past ten years; in return, it provides Japan with much of the tropical hardwood it needs. However, despite the political importance of ODA, Japan has been cutting the amount given since 1999. Then, it stood at about US$11 billion, but by 2003 the amount had fallen to US$8.9 billion. This is a result of the domestic economic problems Japan has been facing. Nevertheless, Japan remains the second biggest ODA donor in the world, after the USA. Japan has also hosted international aid conferences, such as the UN world conference on disaster reduction held in Kobe in 2005, which focused on how to help poorer countries deal with the threats posed by natural disasters.

▲ Containerization has benefited trade in Japan by allowing for the rapid handling and shipping of goods. Within minutes of docking this ship will start unloading.

JAPAN IN THE GLOBAL COMMUNITY

As its economy relies heavily on imported energy and access to world markets, Japan needs to remain on good terms with as many countries as possible. To keep relations with other countries strong, Japan is an active member of a number of global groups and organizations, including the G8 (a group made up of the eight leading industrialized countries in the world), the World Bank, and the Organization for Economic Co-operation and Development (OECD). Japan also takes part in every important international gathering, often in a prominent role. For example, an international conference to tackle climate change was held in Kyoto in 1997. The result was the Kyoto Agreement, which has become the focus for much international debate about the need to reduce greenhouse gas emissions.

 Did you know?

Japan has been a member of the United Nations since 1956. In 2005, the USA supported Japan's application to become a permanent member of the UN Security Council. This would give Japan more influence in discussions of international conflicts and disputes where military intervention or economic sanctions may have to be used.

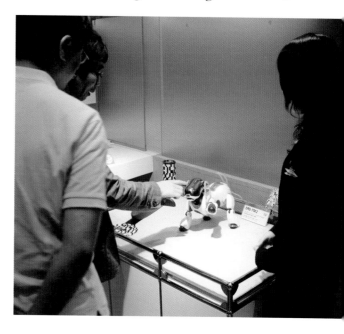

▲ Visitors to a Sony showroom admire Aibo, the robotic dog, one of the latest Japanese electronic products that make up a considerable proportion of the country's exports.

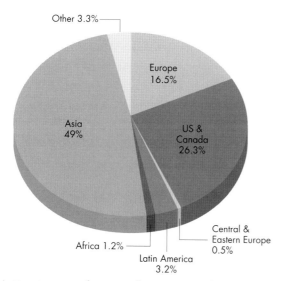

Other 3.3%
Europe 16.5%
Asia 49%
US & Canada 26.3%
Africa 1.2%
Latin America 3.2%
Central & Eastern Europe 0.5%

▲ Destination of exports by major trading region

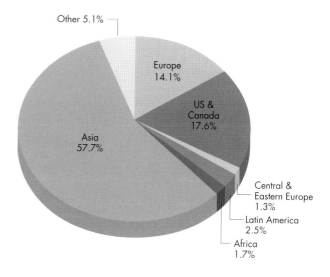

Other 5.1%
Europe 14.1%
US & Canada 17.6%
Asia 57.7%
Central & Eastern Europe 1.3%
Latin America 2.5%
Africa 1.7%

▲ Origin of imports by major trading region

▲ Universal Studios in Osaka is one of several American style theme parks in Japan. It represents the close ties between Japan and the USA.

Since 2001, the Japanese government has further extended Japan's involvement in the global community. Japan's long-term alliance with the USA is partly the reason for this. Since the end of the Second World War, the USA has provided a military shield (see page 25) for the defence of Japan and, from 2004, has worked with Japan on developing a missile defence system. The two countries often work together on foreign policy issues, for example, on how to deal with perceived security threats from North Korea. Japan's concerns about its neighbour were heightened in 1998, when North Korea fired a medium-range missile over Japan and into the Pacific. Since then, Japan and the USA, along with China, Russia and South Korea, have met with North Korea several times to try to convince North Korea to give up its nuclear programme in return for economic aid and guarantees of security. So far, there has been no progress and it is this situation that has led some to argue that Japan needs to arm itself.

Relations with neighbouring countries are politically and economically significant, but they are also stormy. There are ongoing territorial disputes, and resentment against Japanese conduct during the Second World War frequently flares up. For example, in 2005, China and South Korea reacted angrily to the Japanese Ministry of Education's approval of history text books that omitted reference to wartime atrocities committed by Japanese soldiers. But there are also positive connections, including the fact that many of the tourists who visit Japan come from within this East Asian region.

POPULAR CULTURE, TECHNOLOGY AND SPORTS

During the past fifty years or so, the West has strongly influenced Japanese culture. There has been a huge increase in the availability of fast food, such as hamburgers; US leisure activities, most notably baseball, have been widely adopted. South Korean food, music, actors and television 'soaps' are also popular in Japan.

There has also been a growing interest in Japanese culture from outside Japan. *Judo* and *kendo* have gained Olympic status, while *karaoke* singing and collecting *Pokemon* cards have keen followings worldwide. Some types of Japanese food have become very popular in the USA and UK; particularly widespread are *sushi* bars, offering a range of dishes based on rice and raw fish. Also, Japanese manufacturers have played a leading role in the production of games consoles (for example, *Nintendo*), photocopiers and digital technologies, such as cameras and DVDs.

Japan has played an increasingly prominent role in international sport, hosting the Winter Olympics in 1998 and co-hosting (with South Korea) the 2002 Football World Cup. The next major event that Japan will host

is the Rugby World Cup in 2011. Some Japanese baseball players have become famous outside Japan by playing for Major League teams in the USA. Hideki Matsui, for example, has joined the New York Yankees, and Ichiro Suzuki plays for the Seattle Mariners.

▲ Ryoko Tamura of Japan (in white) during her contest to defeat Feng Gao of China and become world *judo* champion at the 2003 championships held in Osaka.

Focus on: Japan's changing relationship with China

Until recently, Japan was the most powerful nation in East Asia. But the balance of power is shifting as China's economy grows. In the past few years, China has begun to compete with Japan for regional influence and resources, particularly energy. Although they are major trading partners, diplomatic relations between them have deteriorated. A number of political issues have given rise to tensions. For example, many in Japan see China's increase in military spending as a threat, while China fears that Japan is abandoning its pacifist stance and drawing closer to the USA to help contain China's growing regional influence. Many Chinese feel that Japan has still not shown remorse about Second World War atrocities and there is widespread anti-Japanese feeling. However, some experts believe it suits the Chinese government to use Japan as a scapegoat because it distracts attention from China's own domestic issues, such as the growing inequality in income.

CHAPTER 9

Transport and Communications

Despite the difficulties posed by its mountainous terrain, Japan has good transport links and Japanese engineers are expert at building bridges and tunnels. Transport networks must also be constructed in a way that minimizes the impact of possible earthquakes. Overall Japan has spent a great deal of money on increasing accessibility across the country. However, in some areas, particularly rural ones, the roads often go nowhere. This is because they were built as part of large schemes allegedly set up by LDP politicians in order to win votes. The roads were not needed, but they provided jobs in the construction industry.

RAIL AND ROAD

Japan is famous for its high-speed trains known as *shinkansen*, or bullet trains. The national rail network includes ordinary trains as well as *shinkansen*. It is extensive, and carries more than 21 billion passengers a year. In 1988 the four main Japanese islands were joined by rail with the completion of a tunnel linking Honshu with Hokkaido, and a bridge linking Honshu with Shikoku. Rail lines linking cities with their suburbs are particularly well used, with more than 70 per cent of office workers in the main cities using them. In nine cities these commuter lines connect with subway lines, enabling people to continue their journey by rail within the city.

The road network is made up of expressways, major roads linking towns and cities and ordinary roads. Expressways link the main cities and, like railways, cross difficult terrain and are built to withstand earth tremors. Not surprisingly, overall construction costs for the expressways are among the highest in the world, and tolls are charged for using them. Over 95 per cent of Japan's freight is transported by road. In the 1960s, car ownership began to increase in Japan, brought about by higher incomes and improvements in roads. Japan also began producing smaller, fuel-efficient cars to suit the domestic situation (fuel is expensive because oil has to be imported, so Japanese cars

▼ Akashi Kaikyo suspension bridge provides a vital transport link between Honshu and Awaji-shima islands. At 3,910 m (12,828 ft), it is the longest suspension bridge in the world.

need to be fuel-efficient). Car ownership continues to rise. In 1990, around 35 million Japanese people owned cars; by 2002 this figure had increased to over 54 million.

Tokyo suffers from serious problems of traffic congestion and air pollution caused by vehicle emissions. Strict regulations have been brought in, particularly in relation to vehicle exhaust emissions. Vehicles are tested regularly to ensure that their emissions of nitrogen oxide (Nox) do not exceed a certain level. However, although individual vehicles now emit much less Nox than used to be the case, the increase in the number of cars on the road means that Nox levels in the atmosphere have worsened.

Transport & communications data

- Total roads: 1,171,647 km/728,048 miles
- Total paved roads: 903,340 km/ 561,325 miles
- Total unpaved roads: 268,307 km/ 166,723 miles
- Total railways: 23,577 km/miles
- Major airports: 174
- Cars per 1,000 people: 428
- Mobile phones per 1,000 people: 679
- Personal computers per 1,000 people: 382
- Internet users per 1,000 people: 483

Source: World Bank and CIA World Factbook

Focus on: Bullet trains (*shinkansen*)

Japan was the first country to develop a high-speed rail system with dedicated track. The first section of high-speed track was opened in 1964, with the first trains running at speeds of up to 200 km/h (125 mph). There have been different models of train built since then, and now they regularly run at speeds up to 300 km/h (185 mph). Called *shinkansen* in Japan (meaning 'New Trunk Line') the trains can be up to sixteen carriages long. The *shinkansen* service is very efficient and reliable. In 2003, the average arrival time was within six seconds of the scheduled time. The track and overhead wires (carrying the electricity that powers the trains) are monitored regularly by high-speed test trains with special equipment. These run during the night so that they do no disrupt the daytime services.

◀ Japan's bullet trains have been copied across the world for their high speed and efficiency. They provide passengers with a high level of comfort and nearly always run full.

AIR AND SEA

Between the 1980s and 2000, air transport grew significantly, with a tripling of the numbers of international passengers entering Japan. But various factors, including economic recession and the threat of terrorism, led to a 9 per cent decrease between 2000 and 2001. Fears about a new contagious disease (SARS) and the continuing threat from terrorism prompted a further decrease in 2003.

The top destinations for Japanese travellers are the USA, China and South Korea. Meanwhile, numbers of those flying within Japan have more than doubled during the past twenty years. The most heavily travelled domestic route is Tokyo-Sapporo. In the past ten years, airports have expanded to meet demand. The largest is New Tokyo International, about 60 km (37 miles) outside Tokyo, which handles more than 30 million passengers and 2 million tonnes of freight a year.

Japan is surrounded by sea, so marine transport has traditionally been important and there are huge port facilities. Until the oil crises in the 1970s, virtually all imports and exports were transported by sea. Increases in costs, and changes in industrial demand towards lightweight technological components mean that some international freight is now transported by air.

 Did you know?

Chubu Centrair international airport near Tokonamo City opened in February 2005. It is the newest of three international airports in Japan and is built on an artificial island. The island is constructed in the shape of a 'D', so that sea currents inside Ise Bay flow freely round it. Also the shores are partially constructed with natural rocks and sloped to allow coastal habitats to develop on them, as they would on the naturally occurring rocky shores found in this area.

▼ Kansei international airport serves the cities of Osaka, Kyoto and Kobe in southern Japan. It is one of Japan's main airports and is built entirely on land reclaimed from the sea.

COMMUNICATIONS AND INFORMATION

The rate at which communications technology is being adopted in Japan has accelerated over the past ten years. Mobile phone ownership has risen from four million in 1995 to over 86 million in 2003. The Internet, which came into commercial use in Japan in 1993, is widely used by more than 77 million individuals in Japan. 88 per cent of all households have Internet access. Within the population, the 13-19 age group has the highest rate of use, with over 91 per cent. The government wants to promote the use of high-speed Internet in schools. It also wants to improve information literacy among the general population by installing terminals in public facilities. The number of subscribers to high-speed connection services has grown particularly fast since 2001, and Japan now has the third highest number of high-speed subscribers in the world, following the USA and South Korea.

Japan has one of the highest newspaper circulations in the world, with 50 million sold each day. There are five general daily papers, including *Yomiuri Shimbun* and *Asahi Shimbun*, and three English language dailies, including the *Japan Times*. Newspapers tend to be delivered to homes or offices rather than bought from shops or stalls. Television ownership is very high and there are many channels on offer. These can be received via three types of networks – through an aerial, a cable or a satellite dish. Recent developments include the promotion of digital broadcasting. The government aims to switch from analogue to digital by 2011.

▲ The latest mobile phones offering Internet and other information services are everywhere in Japan.

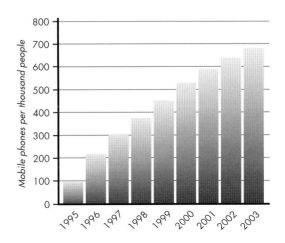

▲ Mobile phone use, 1995-2003

Did you know?

Channel 2 is Japan's most popular website, with comments posted by more than one million people every day. It provides people with the opportunity to highlight news that does not get a mention in the mainstream media. People also have the chance to express their feelings about their lives and may do so anonymously if they wish.

CHAPTER 10

Education and Health

The 1947 School Education Act defined the structure of today's education system in Japan. It established that schooling is compulsory from the ages of 6 to 15. Children spend the first six years at elementary school and then move on to junior high school. After this, students must pass a competitive entrance exam if they wish to attend senior high school. In 2003, 97 per cent of junior high graduates passed this exam. After three years at senior high school, students may go on to higher education. They can choose from a range of different institutions including colleges of technology, which offer vocational courses, and universities, which offer more academic courses. In 2003, about 46 per cent of senior high school graduates moved on to these institutions. Students not going to college or university may enter employment, although during the recession years of the 1990s the number of jobs available to them fell and they suffered higher unemployment than college and university graduates. University graduates tend to have better career opportunities, for example, as research scientists, doctors, lawyers and accountants.

CONTROVERSY AND CHANGE IN EDUCATION

The national curriculum outlines what is to be taught in schools, and this is revised every ten years. The type of text books used in schools is regulated by the Ministry of Education, Culture, Sports, Science and Technology, with the aim of standardizing educational provision across the country. This gives the Ministry a lot of power over what material is considered 'suitable' for students to study. In 2005, the Ministry's approval of a history text book, to be used in Japanese schools, led to a heated international argument. This particular book made no reference to brutal acts carried out by Japanese soldiers against the citizens of China and South Korea during the 1930s and 1940s. Even though many Japanese schools shunned the book, people in China and South Korea were outraged.

Traditional educational values and practices emphasize conformity, rote learning and group discipline rather than individual performance.

◀ A typical elementary school class. Schools are well equipped and Japan has a high standard of education.

There is little scope for students to pursue their interests because the curriculum is pre-determined and testing of achievement is very rigid. However, there are signs that this may be changing. Some high schools are allowing students to choose some of the courses they want to study. At the moment this choice is only available to students in schools serving poorer areas with relatively high truancy rates and low academic results. If it proves successful, however, it may provide the basis for wider changes.

There is a growing demand for equality between the sexes in education. In 1998, 26 per cent of young women went on to university (compared with 15 per cent in 1990), but this was still lower than the 35 per cent of young men who enrolled in 1998. During the recent recession, women graduates found it harder than men to find employment. Also, the career path is much shorter for women than for men because women often have to leave paid employment when they have children. When their children are older they may wish to return to paid employment but are often forced to take lower paid and less satisfying jobs. Older women may then have to leave their jobs again to care for their own, and often their husbands', elderly parents.

 Did you know?

In 2002, the Japanese school week was reduced from six days to five, to give young people more free time in which to pursue their own interests.

Education and health

- 🗀 Life expectancy at birth male: 78.2
- 🗀 Life expectancy at birth female: 85.3
- 🗀 Infant mortality rate per 1,000: 3
- 🗀 Under five mortality rate per 1,000: 4
- 🗀 Physicians per 1,000 people: 2
- 🗀 Health expenditure as % of GDP: 7.9%
- 🗀 Education expenditure as % of GDP: 3.6%
- 🗀 Primary net enrolment: 100%
- 🗀 Pupil-teacher ratio, primary: 20
- 🗀 Adult literacy as % age 15+: n/a

Source: United Nations Agencies and World Bank

◄ These high school students are enjoying an annual sports day. Most Japanese schools hold such days as a highlight of the sporting year. Teams of children compete in sports events and perform artistic displays.

Although education is highly valued by government and society in general, it does not determine success within society, which is still strongly influenced by gender and the social class of parents. The changing of cultural norms (particularly the shift away from the notion of the importance of the group towards that of the individual), advances in science and technology and economic globalization are all challenges the Japanese education system will have to address in the future.

TRENDS IN HEALTH

Japanese women now have the highest life expectancy at birth of any population in the world. In 1970, females had a life expectancy of 74; in 2003, this had risen to 85. The figures for men have also risen over the same period, from 69 to 78. Japan now has the third highest overall life expectancy in the world, after Iceland and Hong Kong. The increases are mainly a result of the development of a well-equipped and comprehensive medical service and advances in medical technology. Over the past fifty years there have been changes in the major causes of death in Japan – from tuberculosis in 1950 to cancer and heart disease in 2005. There is evidence to suggest that increases in cancer and heart disease are linked to lifestyle habits such as smoking (30 per cent of adults smoke, compared with 17 per cent in the USA) and eating fast foods, like burgers and fries, which are high in fats. However, the traditional diet (based around fish, and low in fats

▼ A *sushi* bar in Tokyo: the Japanese diet is traditionally a healthy one, but this is changing as fast foods become more popular, especially with younger generations.

and sugars) is healthy and probably accounts for the low obesity rate in Japan. In 2003, only 3.6 per cent of the adult population was classified as obese, compared with 23 per cent in the UK and 31 per in the USA.

Japan's healthcare system is financed by health insurance and run by the government. It was established in 1961, and all adults participate, mainly through employers' schemes or local authority schemes for the retired. It has generally been very successful, but will be put under strain in the future as a result of the ageing population – 25 per cent of the population will be over 65 by 2020. One government proposal is that specific health insurance schemes are set up for those over a certain age. Older people often need care (for example, having their food cooked and their washing done for them) rather than medicines or operations.

With the traditional role of women in families changing, the pressures on the government to tackle care of the elderly look set to increase.

▶ An 81-year-old man checks his blood pressure in hospital using a self-test machine.

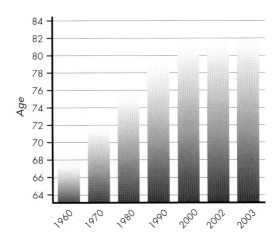

▲ Life expectancy at birth 1960-2003

Focus on: 'Minamata Disease'

During the 1960s, a number of cases of industrial pollution caused deaths or serious health problems. Perhaps the best known of these cases is that of Minamata Bay, where between 1932 and 1968 a local company dumped mercury into the ocean. During this period about 100,000 local people, for whom fish from the Bay was a staple food, became ill with symptoms of mercury poisoning including slurred speech and involuntary spasms in the legs and arms, and many died. It was not until 1968 that the source of 'Minamata Disease' was recognized. The company was taken to court in 1969. Since this case, Japan has become more aware of the dangers of uncontrolled industrial pollution and laws, such as the 1970 Waste Management and Public Cleansing Law, have been passed to prevent the dumping of toxic wastes.

CHAPTER 11

Culture and Religion

Japanese culture is a rich blend of traditional Asian and modern Western influences. The Western trends generally date from the Second World War, when lifestyles changed significantly and many people moved into cities to work in factories and offices. This fundamental change in economic conditions has affected Japanese culture in many ways.

ARCHITECTURE

Historically, Japanese architecture was influenced by Chinese styles. The main building material was wood. The oldest wooden structures in the world date from 670 AD and can be found at the Buddhist temple in Horyuji. Traditional wooden Japanese houses are often constructed on pillars to allow the air to circulate underneath. This keeps the houses cool, particularly in the south of the country with its hot, humid summers. The interior space of these houses is open; opaque paper-covered sliding panels are used to divide the space when necessary. Straw mats, called *tatami*, provide a floor covering that is cool in the summer, warm in winter and fresher than carpet in the humid months. Today, modern houses, especially in cities, are likely to be built of concrete and to have interior walls, but many still have a *tatami* mat room, which is used for peaceful relaxation. Public buildings in cities tend to be modern, high-tech and multi-storeyed, so that maximum use is made of the limited urban space. Many of them date back to

▼ People pray during a service at Higashi Honganjii, a Buddhist temple in Kyoto. The floor is covered with traditional *tatami* mats made of straw. Shoes must be removed to walk on a *tatami* floor.

the end of the Second World War, when the need to rebuild meant that architects and planners could use readily available new materials such as steel, glass and concrete rather than traditional materials.

DRESS AND CUISINE

Traditional dress for men, women and children is the *kimono*. This is usually made from silk, has long sleeves, falls to the ankle, and is tied around the waist with a wide belt called an *obi*. Women's *kimonos* are more elaborate than men's, consisting of twelve separate pieces that

▲ Traditional Japanese dress such as the *kimono* is still worn by some women, but the majority of Japanese people wear Western style clothing today.

have to be put on in a particular order. There is a lightweight, more informal *kimono*, called *yukata*, which may be worn by children. Today, *kimonos* are worn mainly on ceremonial occasions, such as weddings, while Western style clothes (T-shirts, jeans, skirts, dresses, etc.) are more commonly worn for everyday use.

Japanese cuisine is dominated by white rice; all other foods served with it, such as fish, meat or vegetables, are regarded as side dishes. Different traditional cooking techniques, such as grilling or simmering, are used to prepare these side dishes, but some, like *sashimi* (fish), are just left raw. Seafood is very popular; other specialities include *sushi* (rice with raw fish), *miso* soup, *tempura* and pickled vegetables. The traditional diet has been affected by Western influences, which means that items such as pasta, noodles and bread are common. Fast food is also widely available.

 Did you know?

Traditional Japanese meals are named after the number of side dishes, for example, *ichiju-sansai* (one soup, three side dishes).

MUSIC AND THE PERFORMING ARTS

Japan's tradition of classical music dates from the seventh century. This music is played on instruments such as the lute-like *shamisen*, and the *koto*, which is like a zither. More recently, imported Western classical music has become popular. Japan now has some world-class classical musicians, such as the conductor Ozawa Seiji. Traditional folk songs are now less popular among the Japanese, and the ability to play traditional instruments (and the liking of their sound) has fallen away.

Conversely, Japanese and Western popular music has a huge following in Japan. Western pop music was introduced following the Second World War, and from it developed a brand of Japanese pop that uses the pentatonic scale to produce the easy melodies of the West.

RELIGIOUS BELIEFS

Japan has two principal religions – Shintoism and Buddhism. These have co-existed with each other since the introduction of Buddhism in the sixth century. Shinto beliefs and traditions existed before this but, unlike other major religions, there were no written scriptures. Buddhism provided a more formal framework of doctrine, but still permitted the belief in a number of gods that is central to Shintoism. A particular form of Buddhism, called Zen, has developed in Japan. Zen Buddhism emphasizes self-discipline and meditation. Today, 94.6 per cent of Japanese people say they believe in both these religions, although religious practice is not widespread. However, many people use religious ceremonies to celebrate births, marriages and deaths and to mark the New Year.

In 1549, Francis Xavier, a Jesuit missionary, brought Christianity to Japan. At first Japan's ruler, Toyotomi Hideyoshi, tolerated it. But by 1614 the number of Christians had grown to more than 300,000 and the shogun, Tokugawa Ieyasu, became concerned about its popularity. There followed two hundred years of persecution, and it was only in 1859 that Christianity became accepted again. Since then, Christians have swelled in number to more than three million. Christianity is not, however, compatible with the two traditional religions because it does not allow worship of more than one god.

▲ Senso-ji in Tokyo is one of the most visited Buddhist temples in Japan and dates back to the mid-seventh century. Like many Buddhist temple complexes in Japan, it also has a Shinto shrine.

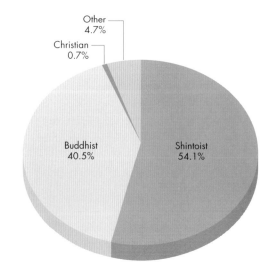

Other
4.7%

Christian
0.7%

Buddhist
40.5%

Shintoist
54.1%

▲ Japan's major religions

► The colourful drama of *Kabuki* theatre remains popular in Japan and has become a major tourist attraction. Actors create and apply their own make-up according to traditional methods.

A noticeable trend since the late 1980s has been the rise in the number of religious cults. A cult is usually founded by one individual who promotes himself as a living deity and whose followers revere his teachings. In 1995, concerns that some cults may pose a threat to Japanese society were raised when members of a cult called Aum Shinrikyo released poison gas in the subways of Tokyo, killing twelve people and injuring more than 5,000. The leader of the cult, Shoko Asaharato, was arrested and sentenced to death for murder in 2004.

 Did you know?

Noh is the oldest form of musical theatre in Japan. It tells a story through dialogue, song and dance. The actors dress in colourful costumes and use decorated masks to switch between characters.

Focus on: The tea ceremony

The Japanese tea ceremony involves the preparation and serving of green tea in the presence of guests, and is a traditional ritual embodying the principles of Zen Buddhism. The main objective of the ceremony is to become completely focused on the actions of the tea-maker and the utensils being used, so that all present are 'living in the moment' rather than having thoughts of other things and places. Participants believe that this state of mind is spiritually uplifting and allows them to appreciate the sacred in everyday actions and objects. Few formal tea ceremonies are performed in Japan today, but many Japanese people attend tea schools to learn these valued traditional skills.

CHAPTER 12

Leisure and Tourism

Leisure time has increased significantly over the past ten years or so. A two-day weekend has been established (instead of just one day) and the number of public holidays has increased (although Japanese employees only take about half their holiday allowance because there is still a cultural expectation to work long hours). Also, in 1997, an amendment to the Labour Standards Law resulted in a reduction in the number of overtime hours worked.

Some families spend a lot of time together, although many fathers still see little of their children because of pressures of work. Family leisure time is spent either at home, watching TV and playing computer games, or on trips out, for example, to one of the many theme parks or to take part in sporting activities such as baseball and swimming.

Annual events, most of which have a traditional importance, provide opportunities throughout the year for Japanese families to celebrate with one another. For example, when the cherry trees flower in April, many families picnic under them and admire the blossom. At the *O-bon* festival (a Buddhist tradition) in August, the souls of ancestors are welcomed into homes where fires are lit to greet them. Many businesses close down at this time and people travel back to their family homes to celebrate *O-bon* together.

▼ The Tokyo Dome is one of the largest baseball stadiums in Japan and attracts sell-out crowds for the major leagues' games.

LEISURE ACTIVITIES

Sports activities tend to be male-dominated, and include jogging, soccer and table tennis. Sports are very popular – jogging has more than two million participants and table tennis more than one million. Winter sports are also popular, particularly skiing and, more recently, snowboarding. There are a number of mountain resorts for these activities in the Japanese Alps and in Hokkaido.

Sporting facilities are generally good – the world's largest artificial ski slope is situated near Tokyo. All major cities have at least one stadium for spectator sports, such as baseball, which has become one of the most popular sports to watch and play. Baseball was introduced to Japan in 1872 and has been played in schools ever since.

There are now twelve professional teams, including the Yomiuri Giants and the Seibu Lions, who play in the two national leagues. Soccer has become more popular in recent years. The 2002 World Cup was co-hosted by Japan and South Korea, and Japanese interest was extremely high during this time.

Tourism in Japan

- Tourist arrivals, millions: 5.212
- Earnings from tourism in US$: 11,475,000,320
- Tourism as % foreign earnings: 2.2
- Tourist departures, millions: 13.296
- Expenditure on tourism in US$: 36,506,001,408

Source: World Bank

 Did you know?

Comic strips, known as *manga*, are very popular in Japan. *Manga* are published in weekly magazines and generally tell stories. There are many types of *manga* aimed at different audiences. Some can be used to help pre-school children learn to read, while others specialize in jokes and humour for adults.

▼ Japanese comics (*manga*) for sale on a news stand: *manga* are popular with adults and children alike and are sold across the country from convenience stores to dedicated *manga* stores.

▲ Bathers enjoy a hot springs bath (*onsen*) in Kirishima-Yaku national park, Kyushu. The waters are heated by geothermal activity of the nearby Kirishima volcano.

Other leisure interests include *pachinko*, a form of pinball. *Pachinko* arcades are widespread throughout the towns and cities of Japan and the industry is worth over £140 billion. It is a form of gambling and, although for most it is a harmless leisure pursuit, there are some for whom it becomes an addiction and they get themselves into serious debt.

Cinema has tended to lose out to television, but recently a number of animated films made in Japan have proved popular at home and abroad. Particularly successful examples include *The Princess Mononoke*, made in 1997, which attracted audiences in excess of 12 million in Japan, and *Spirited Away*, which won an Oscar for the best animated film in 2003. On television, animated shows (*animes*) are also popular. *Animes* such as *Astro Boy* and *Dragonball Z* have also been exported to other countries, including the USA.

HOLIDAYS AT HOME AND ABROAD

Day trips and holidays in Japan are popular. The varied landscape provides many attractions, with activities that have been developed to exploit it. For example, there are about 3,000 spa resorts, such as Ikaho located 129 km (80 miles) north of Tokyo. People visit the spas to bathe in the hot mineral waters. There are also many theme parks attracting both domestic and foreign visitors. They include Yoshimoto Shotenjai (Laughter Street) in Osaka and Tokyo's Disneyland.

Until recently, increasing numbers of Japanese had been travelling abroad. The top tourist destinations were the USA, China and the South Korea. But over the past six years this trend has slowed as a result of economic recession and world events, such as the attack on the World Trade Center in New York City in September 2001. There are foreign visitors to Japan, although these are relatively few because, until recently, it was too expensive for most tourists. In 2003, Japan had just over 5 million tourists, whereas France had 77 million. Overseas tourists visit Japan to enjoy the variety of scenery (such as mountains and lakes) and to take part in, or observe, cultural events such as the cherry blossom viewing. Most tourists come from nearby Asian countries. For example, in 2003, 28 per cent came from South Korea and 15 per cent came from Taiwan. Next down the list was the USA, with 12 per cent, while tourists from the UK made up only 3.8 per cent and Germany 1.8 per cent of the total.

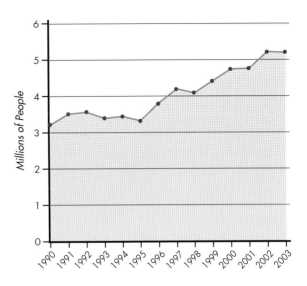

▲ Changes in international tourism, 1990-2003

Focus on: Sumo wrestling

Historical sources show that sumo wrestling has existed in Japan for nearly 2,000 years. In this sport, two men, wearing only colourful *mawashi* (belly bands) wrestle with each other on a floor of sand and clay. Each wrestler aims to make his opponent leave the ring or touch the ground with any part of his body, other than the soles of his feet.

The men, with hair styled like ancient warriors, weigh between 100-280 kg (220-617 lb). All practising wrestlers must belong to a training stable where traditionally they are subject to many rules and regulations about what to eat and how to behave. Although sumo wrestling is still one of the most popular spectator sports, fewer young boys seem to want to take it up today.

This may be because the wearing of the *mawashi* is seen as 'uncool'. It has been suggested that boys should be allowed to wear 'sumo pants', like cycling shorts, but many traditionalists strongly oppose this.

◀ Two wrestlers prepare for a bout at the National Sumo Stadium in Ryogoku, Tokyo.

CHAPTER 13

Environment and Conservation

During the 1960s and 1970s, Japan had very serious pollution problems resulting from rapid industrialization and a belief that economic growth was more important than protection of the environment. Japanese government and businesses seemed unaware of the dangers although, in some cases, even when the damage was obvious, economic growth and profit took priority. In the 1960s, a factory discharged mercury into the Agano River, Niigata, poisoning fish and the local people who ate them. In the same decade, a petrochemical plant in Yokkaiichi released sulphur dioxide, causing high levels of smog and widespread respiratory disease in those living locally.

▲ Emissions from industrial complexes such as this one in Kawasaki add to the problems of air pollution in Japan.

AIR POLLUTION

Since the 1960s, there have been considerable improvements in air and water quality. Measures have been introduced to monitor and control industrial emissions and to manage industrial waste disposal. For example, in 1968, the Air Pollution Control Act was passed and air quality monitoring stations were established. These ensure that levels of pollutants, such as sulphur dioxide, are not exceeded. However, despite such measures, in 2004 Japan was still the world's fourth largest producer of greenhouse gases (after the USA, China and Russia). Urban air pollution is a particular problem, despite the fact that Japan has strict standards to control vehicle emissions by ensuring that vehicles have catalytic converters and use high quality fuel.

WATER POLLUTION

Although many rivers are now cleaner, water quality in lakes and enclosed coastal waters is generally poor, with 25 per cent of lakes and reservoirs affected by algae blooms. These regularly occur when rainfall washes fertilizers off agricultural land. Clean water supplies are limited: the difficulties of building reservoirs where rivers are short and the gradients are steep mean that only 20 per cent of the potential fresh water resources are stored and used. During the period of rapid industrialization in the 1960s, much of the ground water, used for urban supplies was polluted by chemicals used in the manufacture of circuit boards for computers. Over the past decade or so, much of this type of manufacturing activity has relocated

Environmental and conservation data

📁 Forested area as % total land area: 56.7

📁 Protected area as % total land area: 14

📁 Number of protected areas: 770

SPECIES DIVERSITY

Category	Known species	Threatened species
Mammals	188	37
Breeding birds	210	34
Reptiles	92	11
Amphibians	64	10
Fish	1,007	13
Plants	5,565	11

Source: World Resources Institute

to China and South-East Asia. This has led to further decreases in the levels of industrial pollution in Japan.

SUSTAINABLE DEVELOPMENT

The Japanese government is keen to promote sustainability. Laws have recently been introduced to enforce the public and businesses to recycle. In 1997 it became illegal to dump electrical appliances and, in 2005, a similar law was passed to ensure that people dispose of their old cars in an environmentally responsible way. The management of waste in Japan poses a

▼ Car use has increased in Japan, with the number of registered cars on the road rising from 23 million in 1980 to more than 51 million in 2002.

particular challenge, given the lack of space and high density of population. Shortage of space for landfill sites has led to a reliance on incineration, with 78 per cent of waste incinerated. However, public concern over dioxins, which can be released in the burning process, means that it has become increasingly difficult to build more incinerators. However, while Japanese people are concerned about environmental issues such as this, it does not always mean they voluntarily change their behaviour. For example, some households still do not sort their waste into the different recycling bins provided by the authorities for plastics, paper, etc. The Japanese government has begun to emphasize the importance of environmental education. Schools are encouraged to establish junior eco-clubs so students can undertake activities about conservation. Such clubs are offered as an after-school optional extra.

For Japan there is an international dimension to many aspects of sustainability. For example, if fish stocks are to be protected, Japan needs to agree on sustainable practices with neighbouring countries that share the stocks. Japan has, on occasion, been accused of behaving in a non-sustainable way in relation to other countries and shared environments. For example, its use of tropical hardwood has contributed to deforestation in countries such as Malaysia, Papua New Guinea, Gabon and Cameroon. Japan has signed up to some international environmental agreements, for example, the international treaty tackling global warming and climate change, drawn up in Kyoto in 1997. Japan has also signed the Ramsar Convention, indicating a commitment to the protection of wetlands. Since signing this in 1980, Japan has set aside eleven sites, but they tend to be small, some less than 100 hectares (250 acres), and therefore leave much wetland habitat unprotected.

BIODIVERSITY AND CONSERVATION

The range of different habitats found in Japan means that its biodiversity is considerable. The

▲ In Tokyo, municipal waste is separated into different materials and collected on different days at designated collection points. This vehicle is collecting cardboard for recycling.

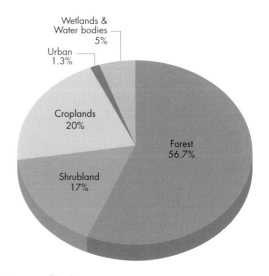

Wetlands & Water bodies 5%
Urban 1.3%
Croplands 20%
Forest 56.7%
Shrubland 17%

▲ Types of habitat

many smaller islands that are part of the Japanese archipelago are home to numerous species, particularly types of fungi and insects that are not found anywhere else in the world. The 'Green Census' is a national inventory that was established by the government in 1973. It lists and monitors details of the natural environment (animals, plants, geology) and is updated every five years. But while 25 per cent of the land area is protected in some way, only 3 per cent is protected specifically for nature conservation. Of Japan's animal and plant species, 20 per cent, including golden eagles and Asiatic black bears, are threatened with extinction. This is because urbanization, intensive agriculture, forestry and recreational activities and facilities have destroyed the habitat. Japan has tried to tackle issues of habitat protection and sustainability through national initiatives such as the Basic Environment Law of 1993, which emphasizes the importance of the conservation of ecosystems.

Focus on: Japan and the international ban on commercial whaling

Japan opposes the international ban on commercial whaling established by the International Whaling Commission (IWC) nearly twenty years ago. At a meeting of the IWC in 2005, Japan led a group of twenty-six nations, out of a total membership of sixty-two, in demanding an end to the ban (75 per cent of countries needed to be in support for the ban to be overturned). Japan argues that fish stocks are threatened by an increasing whale population, that commercial whaling could take place without endangering whale species, and that some rural communities in Japan are suffering hardship because they cannot follow their traditional livelihood of whaling. The eating of whale meat is generally accepted in Japan. The opinions of international scientific experts are divided. Japan continues to hunt whales, killing more than 400 a year for, Japan argues, scientific purposes. Critics of the Japanese position dispute this, partly because the whale meat is sold on for people to eat.

◀ Visitors look out over Ninety-Nine Islands national park north of Nagasaki on Kyushu. It is one of twenty-eight national parks in Japan.

CHAPTER 14

Future Challenges

The recession of the 'lost decade' of the 1990s has made Japan rethink some of its economic practices. In particular, the increasing industrial competition from countries such as South Korea and China has led Japanese companies to focus on the development of 'one of a kind' high-tech products rather than mass produced goods. There have also been political developments. In 2001, Prime Minister Koizumi promised fundamental economic reforms, such as the privatization of the postal system which would enable its fund of savings to be invested in private companies not just state schemes. Until 2005, progress towards reform was slower than promised because many politicians had gained from the state schemes.

ENVIRONMENTAL PRESSURES

Although there has been increasing recognition that the environment is important, pressures on it will continue. As the number of cars increases, air quality deteriorates, despite the fact that all vehicles are now fitted with catalytic converters. Solutions to the waste disposal problem are also urgently needed, and the government is emphasizing the importance of recycling. The challenge facing the Japanese government, in common with all wealthy nations, is the need to protect the environment while still meeting the demands of consumers.

The government faces demands to protect the environment at a time when the economy is still recovering. However, some environmental measures, such as greater energy conservation and the development of alternative energies to oil, could benefit the economy. Japan's continuing dependence on oil imports is clearly problematic, despite the fact that it has been reduced from the 1970s' level. Also, nuclear

◀ Two Japanese red-crested cranes perform a territorial dance in the winter snows of Hokkaido. The protection of endangered species such as this is a considerable challenge for the future.

power is no longer the obvious solution to the energy crisis, as its dangers have been highlighted by recent accidents at nuclear reactors. Further questions about nuclear waste disposal have led to increased public concern.

POPULATION CHANGES

Some see the increase in an ageing population as the greatest challenge Japan faces. This view predicts a health and pension system under strain, and a crisis in the care of the elderly. Traditionally female family members have cared for the elderly but, with more women wishing to work outside the home, this way of life is being eroded. This trend has also contributed to the fact that women are having fewer babies, so there are fewer young people. One way out of the problem might be to see older people as an economic asset. In a prosperous country like Japan they remain fit and healthy far longer than in the past, so perhaps they should be encouraged to continue in productive employment.

JAPAN IN THE WORLD

For the past sixty years, Japan's foreign policy has incorporated a strong pacifist stance, based on its constitution, which forbids the use of military means to deal with international disputes. However, over the past few years there have been signs that Japan is questioning this pacifist principle. In particular, Japan feels threatened by North Korea's military policies and so is starting to look at building up its own military with a missile defence system bought from the USA. With this regional tension, Japan is likely to maintain, and even strengthen, its ties with the USA.

Japan's position as the most economically powerful nation in the East Asian region is increasingly challenged by rapidly developing China. It remains to be seen whether both countries can build a co-operative partnership that is based on their existing strong trade links. At present, China is Japan's biggest trading partner. If their rivalry intensifies, the implications for the future stability and security of the region would be worrying.

▲ The new Fuji Television headquarters in Tokyo were designed by Tange Kenzo, a famous Japanese architect. They are a strong symbol of Japan's continuing modernization and innovation.

Timeline

300 BC-300 AD During the Yayoi Era, ideas brought by migrants from China strongly influence Japanese society.

1192 Minamoto Yoritomo becomes the first ruling shogun.

1549 Christianity is introduced by Jesuit missionary Francis Xavier.

1707 The last recorded eruption of Mount Fuji.

1871 The feudal system is abolished.

1872 Baseball is introduced to Japan.

1889 An Imperial Household Law is passed forbidding women from ascending to the Chrysanthemum Throne.

1914-18 Japan fights on the side of the Allies in the First World War.

1923 The Great Kanto earthquake devastates the Tokyo area.

1937 War between China and Japan escalates into a Pacific War and later becomes part of the Second World War.

1941 Japan launches an attack on the US Navy at Pearl Harbor which prompts the USA to declare war on Japan.

1945 Atomic bombs are dropped on Hiroshima and Nagasaki by the US military.

1947 A new constitution, written by the US occupying power, is established. Women are given the vote.

1964 The first section of high-speed rail track for the bullet trains opens.

1993 The Liberal Democratic Party loses power. It has been the ruling political party in Japan since the 1950s.

1998 Japan hosts the Winter Olympics.

2001 The Liberal Democratic Party is returned to power and Junichiro Koizumi becomes prime minister.

2002 Japan and South Korea co-host the Football World Cup.

2005 Anti-Japanese protests in China and South Korea are sparked by the publication of a Japanese school history text book that omits to mention Japan's wartime atrocities.

2005 The Liberal Democratic Party wins general election with the biggest majority for twenty years.

Glossary

Allies (First World War) The countries, including France, Russia, Britain, Italy and the USA, that fought against Germany in the First World War.

Allied/Allies (Second World War) The countries, including France, the UK, Canada and the USA, that fought against Germany, Italy and Japan in the Second World War.

Analogue A system that uses electrical waves to transmit television services.

Annex To take possession of a country or an area of land, usually by force or without permission.

Annexation The taking possession of a country by another country.

Asian Tigers The Asian countries, including South Korea, Taiwan, Singapore, Hong Kong and China, that have achieved high economic growth by producing large quantities of goods to sell abroad.

Coalition The union of different political parties or groups for a particular purpose, usually for a limited time period.

Communist Someone who believes in a society governed by an economic system without different classes and in which everyone has an equal share in what is produced through agriculture and industry.

Constitution A written document that sets out the political principles by which a nation is governed.

Democratic Describes a system of government based on the principle that all adult citizens should have a say in how the country is governed. This involves citizens being able to vote for people to represent them in government.

Digital A system that converts sound and pictures into digital form and transmits them very quickly. It is believed that digital transmission is more efficient than analogue in delivering TV services.

Dioxins Poisonous chemicals that are released when certain substances such as plastics are burned.

Dutch East India Company A trade organization established in the Netherlands in 1602 to carry out foreign trading, particularly with the Dutch colonies but also with independent countries such as Japan.

Edo era An era of Japanese history named after the capital city of the time, now renamed Tokyo.

Expansionism The act of increasing the amount of land ruled over by a country, often by force.

G8 A group of the eight leading industrialized countries in the world. The G8 meets every year to discuss issues of global importance, for example, the fight against AIDS.

Geothermal Referring to the heat inside the earth.

Greenhouse gas emissions The release of gases, from human activity and natural processes, into the earth's atmosphere. These then absorb and trap the heat from the sun, keeping it in the atmosphere. The emissions include carbon dioxide, methane and nitrous oxides.

Hereditary Describes a process by which titles and positions in society are passed from parent to child.

Hierarchy A system in which people are arranged according to their importance.

Homogenous Similar, or of the same type.

Indigenous Original or native to an area or country.

Manchuria A large area of approximately 200,000 sq km (77,220 sq miles) in the north-east of Asia, within the borders of China.

Nationalism Loyalty or devotion to one's country – extreme nationalists believe that their country is better than all others.

Pentatonic scale A musical scale consisting of five notes.

Precipitation Water falling from clouds, usually in the form of rain or snow.

Prefectures Political districts of Japan, like states or counties.

Representative government Government which speaks for the people, who have had some influence in choosing its members.

SARS (Severe Acute Respiratory Syndrome) A particularly dangerous form of pneumonia that first appeared in China in 2002. It spreads rapidly and many people have died from it.

Seismically Relating to or caused by earthquakes.

Shogun The name given to the rulers of Japan between 1192 and 1868.

Sustainability A way of life and a means of economic development that can be carried on at the same level into the future without damaging the environment.

Tectonic plates The large rigid blocks that make up the surface of the earth's crust.

Tsunami A giant sea surge affecting coastal areas, triggered by earth movements or volcanic eruptions under the sea.

United Nations (UN) An international organization established after the Second World War in 1945 to work towards maintaining international peace and security, and international economic and social co-operation.

UN Security Council Part of the UN, the Security Council has the particular focus or aim of maintaining peace between nations.

Yayoi era An era of Japanese history named after the area of Tokyo in which archaeological investigations uncovered the first recognized traces of this period.

Further Information

BOOKS TO READ

Hiroshima (Days that Shook the World series)
Jason Hook
(Hodder Wayland, 2003)

Japan (Changing Face of... series)
L. Lansford, C, Scharz
(Hodder Wayland, 2004)

Japan (Culture in... series)
M. Guile
(Heinemann, 2003)

Japan (Nations of the World series)
Jen Green
(Raintree, 2004)

Manga Madness
D. Okum
(North Light Books, 2004)

Pearl Harbor (Days that Shook the World series)
Paul Dowswell
(Hodder Wayland, 2002)

USEFUL WEBSITES

www.eia.doe.gov/emeu/cabs/japanenv.html
www.eia.doe.gov/emeu/cabs/japan.html
Two detailed country profiles of Japan provided
by the US Department of Energy and with a
particular focus on energy, and energy and the
environment.

www.economist.com/countries/Japan
A country briefing and articles from the journal
The Economist.

www.state.gov/p/eap/
The East Asian and Pacific section of the US
Department of State website. From this site,
background notes of Japan can be accessed via
the Countries and Other Areas button or by
clicking on Japan on the map.

http://web-japan.org/factsheet
A site sponsored by Japan's Ministry of Foreign
Affairs, providing information on many aspects
of Japan. It includes a section for children.

www.stat.go.jp/english/index.htm
A site provided by Japan's Ministry of Internal
Affairs and Communication, presenting many
statistics about Japanese society, including up-
to-date figures from the *Japan Statistical
Yearbook* and some commentary on these in the
Statistical Handbook of Japan.

www.earthtrends.org/
A range of statistics on different aspects of the
environment available for selected countries,
including Japan.

www.odci.gov/cia/publications/factbook/
Select Japan for CIA facts and figures on Japan.

www.unicef.org/infobycountry/japan.html
UNICEF's website provides a country profile of
population statistics focusing on children.

Index

Page numbers in **bold** indicate pictures.

About the Author

Celia Tidmarsh is a geography PGCE tutor at the Graduate School of Education, University of Bristol. She has taught geography in secondary schools in the UK for fifteen years.

She has written a number of geography text books on various topics for young people, and has also carried out research into children's attitudes to nature and environmental issues.